ACACIA TERRACE

Library of Congress Cataloging-in-Publication Data

Wilson, Barbara Ker, 1929–
Acacia Terrace.

Summary: Traces the history of Acacia Terrace in
Sydney, Australia, through the lives of one family
living there from the 1860s to after World War II.
1. Acacia Terrace (Sydney, N.S.W.)—History—Juvenile
literature. 2. Sydney (N.S.W.)—Social life and customs
—Juvenile literature. 3. Dwellings—Australia—Sydney
(N.S.W.)—History—Juvenile. 4. Sydney (N.S.W.)—History
—Juvenile literature. [1. Acacia Terrace (Sydney,
N.S.W.)—History. 2. Sydney (N.S.W.)—Social life and
customs] I. Fielding, David, 1944–   ill. II. Title.
DU178.W48 1988   994.4'1   89-10359

ISBN 0-590-42885-3

12 11 10 9 8 7 6 5 4 3 2 1   9/8 0 1 2 3 4/9
Printed in the U.S.A.   36
First Scholastic printing, February 1990

ACACIA TERRACE

by Barbara Ker Wilson   Illustrated by David Fielding

SCHOLASTIC INC.   NEW YORK

THE story of Acacia Terrace is about people and lifetimes, houses and history. It begins long before Acacia Terrace was even thought of, and far away from Sydney, Australia, where it was built.

◆ ◆ ◆

A hot day in 1855, on the Emu Gully goldfield in Victoria . . .

Rose Robson trudged down to the creek and flopped in the shade of a wattle tree heavy with blossoms.

Rose looked at the goldfield around her. The dusty landscape was dotted with calico tents and alive with toiling bodies. The stillness of the day was shattered as a flock of parrots screeched across the sky. Rose groaned. "I hate eating parrot pie every night and I hate living in a tent," she told herself.

She leaned back in the dry grass, cradled her head in her arms and dreamed of a house in England, with a front and back door, windows and a cobbled street outside. Suddenly the house was gone. A clipper ship on a stormy sea pitched and tossed into Rose's dream. Rose was sucked into a whirlpool of images, a seventy day journey compressed into a split second. The images spun faster and faster.

"Help!"

A firm hand on her shoulder pulled her back into reality.

"Michael! I was dreaming of home. Do you ever do that?"

Michael Flynn scratched his head. "Australia is home to me, Rose. I was born here. Our family left Ireland to escape the terrible potato famine. We won't go back."

Rose looked at the golden wattle blossom contrasted against the clear blue sky. The pungent smell of eucalyptus trees wafted over her and in the distance she heard a kookaburra laughing.

"You know, Michael, I don't think I really want to go home. All I really want, is to live in a proper house again."

Michael drew patterns in the dust with a stick.

"I'll tell you what, Rose. If you do stay in Australia, one day, when we're grown-up, I'll build you the best house you've ever seen."

THE Flynns stayed on the goldfield, still hoping to strike it lucky one day, and the Robson family went to live in Sydney.

As the years went by, Rose often wondered what had happened to Michael Flynn.

◆ ◆ ◆

A few days after her eighteenth birthday, Rose was at a church social. She heard a voice close behind her.

"Hello Rose."

Rose half-turned.

"I don't believe it! Michael Flynn! What are you doing in Sydney?"

"Well, my father found enough gold at Emu Gully to buy some land and set himself up as a farmer. I helped him build a house. It was only very small with log walls, mud plaster, hard earth floor and a cast iron roof, but it was ours. I decided then, I wanted to learn the building trade. That's why I'm in Sydney."

"And when are you going to build me the best house I've ever seen?"

"When you marry me, Rose Robson."

◆ ◆ ◆

Two years later, Michael and Rose were married. Rose's wedding ring was made from a little piece of the gold Michael's father had found at Emu Gully.

Their first home was a white cottage with a red roof and a picket fence, next door to the general store. They rented the cottage from the doctor whose house stood a little way up the hill.

This corner of Sydney was close by the harbor. The few houses near the Flynns had a harbor view across the land in front of them, which was used as a pasture for sheep.

There was a lot of building taking place in Sydney. Soon Michael was able to set up his own business.

By 1872, five years later, Rose and Michael Flynn had a family of four little girls: Louisa, Emily, Alice and Kate. By now the cottage had become far too small for them, and when the doctor died, Michael bought his house and all the land that lay between it and the general store.

"Now I can build you a house," Michael said to Rose, "like the one you used to talk about when we were children at Emu Gully. A *proper* house, I think you called it!"

MICHAEL didn't build just one house, he built a terrace of three houses. Each one had a beautiful view of the harbor.

"What shall we call our terrace?" he asked.

"Let me think." Rose's thoughts went back to the goldfield. She remembered the peppery scent of the yellow wattle, golden trees in a landscape of gold. "Why not . . . Acacia Terrace . . . a grand name for a grand terrace!"

"Acacia Terrace it shall be!"

"Oh, Michael, I'm so looking forward to moving in."

"So are we!" cried four excited little voices.

"Just think, we shall each have our own bedroom!" said Louise.

"And a staircase," said Emily, "with a banister to slide down!"

"And the front parlor will have a view of the harbor!" said Alice.

Rose smiled as she looked at Acacia Terrace. She thought of family sing-alongs and musical evenings around the piano in the parlor. And she recalled heat, dust and a childhood promise.

Michael put his arm around her waist, "A penny for your thoughts."

"Well now, I was just thinking . . ."

". . . that I've built you the best house you've ever seen!"

"The best."

A year later, there was great excitement in the Flynn household. A new baby was due.

Michael paced up and down the parlor and looked absently out the window at the harbor.

Suddenly the door burst open. The midwife came bustling in. "Well, Mr. Flynn, congratulations. You have a fine young son!"

Albert was christened in the church on the hill and afterwards the whole family gathered in the parlor to have their photograph taken.

The parlor was the best room in the house, usually kept for company and practicing the piano. (The piano stood in one corner well away from the window, in case the sunlight spoiled its polish.) At night two oil lamps lit the room with a soft glow, and the velvet curtains were drawn against the darkness outside.

After the children had gone to bed, Rose and Michael would often sit in the soft glow of the lamps and enjoy a time of quiet conversation.

"The McPhee and Davis families are good neighbors, Rose. I'm glad we sold them the other two houses."

"The children all seem to enjoy playing together too."

Michael glanced at one of the pictures on the wall. "Do you remember when we had that painted?"

"So many changes have taken place since then. Just think how rough the road used to be. It's certainly a smoother ride in the carriage these days, thank goodness."

Other things had changed too. The sheep pasture in front of Acacia Terrace had been turned into a park, with flower beds and palm trees, a rotunda where a band played on Sunday afternoons, and notices that said "Keep off the Grass."

The girls pushed their toy baby carriages along the paths. The boys flew kites, but they were not allowed to play football or cricket there. Instead they had exciting games of "bushrangers."

"THAT rogue Ned Kelly has been taken prisoner," said Rose. "Whoever captured him deserves a medal from Her Majesty."

Michael smiled and brushed his moustache. "It appears his name is Sergeant Steele of the Wangaratta Police."

"Where's Wangaratta, Father?"

"What happened?"

Louisa, Emily, Alice and Kate gathered excitedly around their father.

"We'll discuss it later. Now off to school with you."

The year was 1880. It became compulsory for every child in New South Wales to attend school. The four Flynn girls already went to a small school for young ladies not far from their home.

These were good times. Acacia Terrace was elegant and well-kept. Other houses were being built around it, and Michael's business continued to grow.

The roads had become much busier. Tradesmen came every day with deliveries of coal and wood, fruit and vegetables, fish, bread, milk and ice.

◆ ◆ ◆

The years passed, and to Rose and Michael it did not seem long before their children were grown-up.

Louisa married William McPhee and Emily married Walter Davis. They moved away from Acacia Terrace to set up homes of their own.

Alice was still at home. Rose hated the thought of her leaving.

Kate made a very definite statement to her parents: "I want to be a teacher!"

"I don't know, Kate."

"Oh, Mother. I'm eighteen."

"Is it what you really want, Kate?"

"Yes, Father."

"Very well. We'll arrange for you to go to teachers' training college."

Albert was rather delicate and had to be careful of his chest; he had a nasty cough. It worried him at times, but did not stop him from going into his father's business and learning the building trade. Michael was proud to call his business "Michael Flynn and Son, Builders."

◆ ◆ ◆

Then, in 1891, hard times came to Australia. There were worldwide money difficulties. Many banks closed down and some people lost all their savings. People could not afford to have new houses built. Michael Flynn and Son felt the pinch.

Acacia Terrace no longer looked as elegant as it used to be.

"THE neighborhood is starting to look shabby, Michael. What is going to happen?"

"I'll tell you what's happening, my dear. It's the evening of the first of January, 1901. Federation* is here, and we are going to celebrate. Come along!"

They walked along a street gaily lit with Chinese lanterns and went to the park to watch the blaze of fireworks over the harbor.

That New Year's day, Michael, Rose, Alice, Kate and Albert, set out early and took a ferry across the harbor to join the crowds in the city.

A great procession passed through the streets to Centennial Park, where the flag of the new Commonwealth of Australia was hoisted to the cheers of the crowd and the boom of a twenty-one gun salute.

"Do you know that a fifteen-year-old schoolboy designed that flag? His name is Ivor Evans," Kate said smugly.

"Now we really are one country," said Michael.

Everyone sang the National Anthem, *God Save the Queen.* But later that month, Queen Victoria died and the anthem changed to *God Save the King* when Edward VII came to the throne.

◆ ◆ ◆

Michael Flynn died in 1910. Rose went on living with Alice and Albert in the house he had built for her. Kate had become a teacher in a little country school.

Louisa and Emily now had children of their own. The children often came to visit their Grandmother Flynn in Acacia Terrace.

Nowadays, automobiles drove past the terrace, and many tradesmen used trucks; though milk and bread were still delivered by horse and cart.

Rose would listen for the clip-clop of the horses' hooves and think to herself that it was comforting some things hadn't changed.

But great changes were on the way and not just in the neighborhood of Acacia Terrace. Changes that would affect Australia . . . and the whole world.

There was talk of war.

*On January 1, 1901, Australia's six independent colonies were united under a new nation, the *Commonwealth of Australia.*

"BRITAIN is at war with Germany, Bertie. Thousands of our men are volunteering to go and fight." Rose looked fondly at Albert. "Thank God you can't go!"

The year was 1914. Australia and New Zealand went to Britain's aid. Part of the Australian and New Zealand Army Corps, the ANZACS, were sent to the Dardanelles, in Turkey, to try to capture the city of Constantinople. They landed at Gallipoli. The heroic attempt failed, but the campaign would become a proud legend.

The ANZACS also fought in the dreadful trench warfare in France. Long casualty lists of the dead and wounded appeared in all the newspapers. The government kept appealing for more soldiers to enlist. Albert Flynn did not volunteer. He was not a young man and often had difficulty breathing.

One day as he was walking down to the park, his way was blocked by a group of women.

"It's Bertie Flynn!"

"He should be wearing a uniform!"

"Have you the . . ." (whisper, whisper.)

"Give it to him now!"

A young woman stepped from the group and thrust a white feather into Albert's hand.

"Here, take it. You shall have a badge — a coward's badge!"

Albert accepted the feather with a mock bow. He took it home. Alice came in the front door as he was placing it in the hall vase.

"Oh, Bertie, a white feather. How awful!"

"I'm not ashamed, Alice. I feel I'm doing my duty by trying to keep Father's business going."

◆ ◆ ◆

Five years later, the war ended with an armistice.

And in 1918, Albert became one of the hundreds of victims of the influenza epidemic that swept Sydney.

After Albert's funeral, Rose and Alice sat in the parlor staring out at the harbor.

"Well Alice, here we are, just the two of us, with a big house and a small income."

"I don't want to move, Mother. The house means so much to me."

"And even more to me, dear girl."

Rose picked up a newspaper and glanced absently at the classified section. Then she looked more closely, and smiled.

"Alice, I have an idea! We'll take in lodgers!"

THE first lodger to move in was a bank clerk, Mr. Smerk. He was a very respectable young man who wore paper cuffs at work to protect his shirts.

The second, Boris Rostropov, a refugee from the 1917 Russian revolution, was far more interesting. He had a gramophone in his bed-sitting room and played sad Russian music. A precious icon hung on his wall, and in one corner stood a rather moth-eaten bear. Boris had found the bear in a secondhand shop in Sydney. He said it reminded him of Russia.

"Isn't it romantic, having a Russian prince as a lodger!" Rose said to Alice.

"Actually Mother, I often wonder if he is a prince. He always has to be reminded about the rent. Personally, I prefer Mr. Smerk. At least he always pays on time."

Eventually Mr. Smerk left Acacia Terrace, and Prince Boris went to America, leaving his bear behind him. After that, there were many other lodgers.

"But none like Prince Boris," Rose said wistfully.

As the years went by, Rose spent more and more time gazing at the harbor from the parlor window. She often thought of heat, dust, wattle blossoms, and a handsome young man.

◆ ◆ ◆

When her mother died Kate retired from teaching and came home to share the old family house with Alice.

"Shall we take in more lodgers, Kate?" Alice asked her sister.

"Definitely not!" Kate replied. "We're not getting any younger. Anyway, I don't want the extra work. Do you?"

"No, but . . ."

"No 'buts' about it. What we need is a holiday. Let's go to Katoomba, in the Blue Mountains!"

At the hotel where they stayed, Kate and Alice met a charming widower, Mr. Sandson. He became particularly fond of Alice.

◆ ◆ ◆

Later that year, Alice and Mr. Sandson were married in the old church not far from Acacia Terrace.

"You'll share the house with me, of course," said Kate.

Alice and her husband laughed. "How can we refuse such an offer?"

The Flynn house was the only one in Acacia Terrace that had not been converted into apartments. The McPhee and Davis families had left long ago, and there seemed to be people coming and going all the time.

DAVID FIELDING 1987

"I wonder how long *they'll* be here." Kate looked out of the window at the couple next door. She could see the wife pointing towards the Flynn house.

A moment later, there was a knock on the front door. Kate went to answer it.

"Good morning, missus. Got any work? I've lost my job you see, and the wife thought . . ."

Before Kate could answer, the man turned away with an embarrassed look on his face. "No, of course you haven't. Sorry to trouble you."

As Kate closed the door, she said to Alice, "Poor things. They can barely scrape together enough money to pay the rent."

A few weeks later they were evicted. Furniture and personal belongings stood on the pavement.

For a while the family huddled together desperately trying to comfort each other. A little while later, they piled their belongings into a cart and trundled off into the distance.

This was the 1930s, the time of the Great Depression. Acacia Terrace looked seedy and decrepit, and the little park had become sadly neglected. Unemployed and homeless people often slept there at night, covering themselves with newspapers to keep warm.

A great bridge now spanned the harbor. One fall day in 1932, Kate, Alice and Mr. Sandson went to the opening of the Sydney Harbor Bridge. Just as the Premier of New South Wales was about to cut the ribbon, a horseman galloped up and slashed it with a sword.

"Probably some sort of political protest," muttered Mr. Sandson.

As they walked back to the city, Kate looked out over the harbor.

"I remember how Mother used to talk about the long sea voyage she made when she was a little girl."

"Over seventy days by sailing ship," remarked Alice.

"These days flying boats take only a week to travel from Australia to Britain," added Mr. Sandson.

An airplane droned overhead carrying passengers across the sky with a flash of silvery wings.

Before long, other planes would flash across the sky, but for a very different purpose.

DAVID FIELDING 1987

"IT'S war!" Mr. Sandson switched off the radio and turned to Kate and Alice. "War has been declared, and Australia has joined the fight!"

It was 1939, the beginning of the Second World War. When Japan became an ally of Nazi Germany and threatened to invade Australia, America came to Australia's aid. Thousands of American servicemen were based in Sydney and other cities and towns of Australia.

The park opposite Acacia Terrace was very popular with the American servicemen. "Such nice young men," Alice said, and often invited them to the house for afternoon tea.

At night, there was a "brownout" all over the city. Mr. Sandson always made sure no chink of light showed from the windows of the house in Acacia Terrace.

"Better to be sure than sorry," he said.

The walls in the neighborhood were plastered with posters that said: CARELESS TALK COSTS LIVES and THE ENEMY IS LISTENING.

"What dreadful times," sighed Alice. "Will peace ever come?"

Peace did come in 1945, with the defeat of Germany and the surrender of Japan after the first atomic bombs were dropped on the cities of Hiroshima and Nagasaki.

◆ ◆ ◆

Soon after the war ended, Mr. Sandson died. Alice and Kate were now very old ladies.

"The house is just too much for us Alice. It's time to decide what we are going to do."

"Well . . . I have heard of a home for elderly folk. It's supposed to be very comfortable."

They took a few treasured possessions with them, including the painting of Acacia Terrace that used to hang on the wall of the parlor. As she wrapped it, Kate said quietly, "This way it will always be with us."

The day they left the house, Kate took one last look at their home. As they stepped into the waiting taxi, she turned to Alice and said, "It's the end of an era, Alice . . . for us, and for Acacia Terrace."

AFTER the war, new people came to live in Acacia Terrace. The Flynn house was divided into apartments, with ever-changing tenants. The other two houses had been reconverted into single dwellings.

Acacia Terrace had become so shabby that the houses were quite cheap to buy.

Some people called Bowden moved into the house that had once belonged to the Davis family. They had one daughter, Shirley.

In the McPhee's old house lived a family that had emigrated from Italy to start a new life in Australia. The Carbonis had five children. The eldest was a son, Mario.

Mr. Carboni painted his old-new house cheerful colors.

"A bit bright aren't they, Papa?" laughed Mario.

"And why not? They are happy colors; we are a happy family and they remind me of Italy!"

◆ ◆ ◆

When television came to Australia in the 1950s, the Carbonis often moved their television set to the front door. They sat on the verandah to watch their favorite programs, enjoying the breeze from the harbor.

At first, the neighbors laughed at them. But, one by one, the television sets in Acacia Terrace crept closer and closer to the doors . . . and the harbor breeze!

"Turn that off Shirley. It's not music, it's just noise!"

"It's the Beatles, Mom. They're a pop group. Aren't they FAB! I'm going to see them tonight."

"You can't go by yourself," declared her father.

"I'm going with Mario Carboni," replied Shirley.

Shirley was glad to have Mario beside her when they were caught up in the screaming, yelling crowd.

"Great, wasn't it?" said Mario, gently holding Shirley's hand.

All the way home they sang *Love Me Do.*

A few years later, they married and moved away from Acacia Terrace.

◆ ◆ ◆

The old Flynn house had seen many people come and go. Some of the present tenants were students. When young Australians were drafted to fight alongside the Americans in the Vietnam War, these students took part in anti-war demonstrations. They held noisy meetings in the room that was once Rose Flynn's front parlor.

The time was the 1960s—"the Age of Aquarius."

THE heavy scent of incense wafted from one of the cottages next to Acacia Terrace. A group of hippies had moved in. They played Indian sitar music and wore badges that said "Make love not war." In the back yard they grew a wide variety of vegetables and other plants.

"All organically grown, no insecticides on these!" they told their neighbors proudly.

"How do you round up the bugs?" teased one old man, winking at his wife.

"Fred used to be a farmer," she explained to the hippies.

They nodded. "Peace," they said, and went inside.

Late one night, there was a loud knock on Fred's door.

"What do you want?" he glared at the frantic figure on the doorstep.

"Please, Fred, phone the fire brigade. Someone left a candle burning on the table when they went to bed. It fell over and . . ."

By the time the fire was extinguished, Acacia Terrace was badly damaged.

The years passed and it grew more and more dilapidated.

The Flynns' former house stood empty and forgotten. It became a target for vandals, and home to stray cats and old men down on their luck.

One day, a car pulled up outside. A young couple climbed out and walked towards the rusty gate.

"We've found it, Tony! I'm sure this is the old family house. Look, it's for sale!"

As they picked their way through the debris in what once was the front garden, Tony Mead said, "Your great-great-great grandfather built Acacia Tererace, didn't he?"

Katherine nodded, "Yes. It remained in the family until great-great Aunt Kate went into a nursing home."

Tony Mead was an architect. He was fascinated by the old place and could imagine how it would look once it was restored.

A few months later, Katherine and Tony Mead bought Acacia Terrace. It took them three years to restore the house that Michael Flynn had built one hundred years ago.

◆ ◆ ◆

A few years later, Acacia Terrace and all the other houses along the street were threatened with demolition.

Tony strode around the kitchen waving the proposal in the air. "High rise units on the park site and an extension of the nearby freeway. It must not happen, Kate."

Katherine Mead smiled grimly. "It won't," she said in a very determined voice.

DAVID FIELDING 1987

Meetings were held and a protest movement was organized: SAVE OUR STREET.

A lively procession was assembled one Saturday afternoon, and radio and television programs spread the news about what might happen in this corner of the city. A group of people concerned with saving historic buildings came to look at the street.

They described the brick house where the doctor had once lived before Acacia Terrace was built as "a perfect example of early colonial architecture," and Acacia Terrace itself as "a fine example of mid-Victorian building."

As a result of all this activity, the demolition proposal was withdrawn.

Katherine and Tony sat in the old rotunda in the park. Katherine looked across the road to Acacia Terrace and said triumphantly, "I think we've won, Tony. We've saved Acacia Terrace."

SAVE OUR STREET

LAN-CHOO TEA
Ceylons, choicest

Peters ICE CREAM

PAUL'S CORNER STORE

COCA COLA ALPINE

BUY NEW IDEA

DAVID FIELDING 1987

THE neighborhood was ecstatic. Not only Acacia Terrace, but the whole street was saved.

The little park was replanted with trees and shrubs and the rotunda where the band used to play was repaired and repainted. The park was so attractive that it became a popular place for bridal parties to be photographed.

City newspapers reported the event in these words:

"An important victory for a small local community determined to beat bureaucratic red tape."

TEN years later Katherine and Tony Mead gave a dinner party to celebrate the tenth anniversary of this victory. Katherine proposed a toast: "Long live Acacia Terrace!"

After their guests had gone, Tony and Katherine sat on the balcony deep in their own thoughts.

Tony was thinking how successful the whole venture had been. He had saved many other historic buildings in the area as well as Acacia Terrace.

Katherine was thinking of what the victory celebration was really all about: people and lifetimes, houses and history.

"It all began long ago," she mused, "long before Acacia Terrace was even thought of, and far away from Sydney . . ."